# Musings and Miracles

AF624554

Maya Marie Coles

BookLeaf Publishing

Presentation by *BookLeaf Publishing*

Web: www.bookleafpub.com

E-mail: info@bookleafpub.com

ISBN: 9789357442336

First edition 2023

# adoring dancing souls

i am knee deep in the sonnets i could write about
every woman i have ever laid eyes on.
all the markings and experience in their skin
when the sun hits it just right.
i wanted to reflect them
i wanted to look them in their eyes
and speak with such delicacy
pronounce my love for them, platonically, in
simple idolization.

if i'm ever caught in a bad night, these feelings
may shift into jealousy
my eyes hazel, green with envy
their eyes brown like a pool of chocolate or
caramel
or blue like neptune or when children draw rain
with crayons.
maybe i'll scrutinize myself in the mirror,
tilting my head back in the shower
so the tiles can't tell the difference between tears
and water.

i wondered what music they danced in their
rooms to
what their favorite flower was

if they ever had a repulsive boyfriend that took
them for granted.
these women were unapologetically
unparalleled.
and i wondered if i would begin to think too
long and too hard about my identity
just because i wasn't a carbon copy of Her. of
any of them.

they say beauty is in the eye of the beholder
but all these eyes of all these beholders must
have some common sense.
admiring from afar, walking with such grace and
felicity,
dressed like they were about to be gifted a
bouquet
or frolic through a meadow.

girls i could never be
but i could be more like.

and i am picturing it as if
maybe, hopefully
someone, somewhere
may be writing the same things about me.

# contradiction

just how guilty are my hands
and just how disturbing are my dreams

my skin crawls of memory
my body a portrait of comparison
strip me down to my core
just how beautiful are my bones?

telling me you love it when i talk
but overthinking and refusing to speak,
that you love the way i touch you
but recalling everyone else who has before me
and removing my fingertips from your freckles.

my tissues are tired
and my heart yearns for the sun
but my mind wants the stars
so my system is dim.
my organs plead for release
the tension, the impulse, the cry
until i am soft and i drift off to sleep
and out comes my nightcrawler, my daydreamer
the source of all my sorrow
and the root of all my revelation.

now at my most vulnerable
my nerves able to calm
my questions unawaringly answered
my stomach settling
my flowers blooming.

now come and touch me, envelop me
i want to speak to you
i've come to terms with the past and the ancestry
the faults amidst our familiarity.
waves of anxiety but an ocean of override
and i am strengthened
one with my body, my peace inner, my world
formed.

# specimen

she dislikes the feeling of prolonged solitude
as much as she does a constant crowd
she is the single glimmer in a field of black
like a diamond upon leather.

eradicating the confinement
she goes to dance outside her door
and stops to smell the roses
whilst encouraging the thorns.

balance is of the utmost importance
and as she puts one foot in front of the other
across the wall of bricks on her front porch
she is prominent in prose.

having never committed a sin
the brisk of innocence flutters through her
fingers
and the envelopment of the sun
showers her in a yellow ecstasy.

perfection is too misused a word
but she was perfectly pertained
not a single flaw from toes to jaw
a figure of femininity.

selective in her words, she'll say
"Oh, you're all too sweet to me"
and although sublime and humble and kind
she was celebrated ceaselessly.

# true

i always keep my flowers longer than their
lifespan
because it is terribly troublesome to let things go
especially if they were a gift from you
reveling in a holiday.

i love the way we speak when there is nothing
meaningful to say
as well as when we're immersed in deep
conversation.
or even when we're not speaking at all,
enjoying just bodies and breaths.

the entanglement of awe
my back arching into you like a crescent moon
the universal figure of affection.
my way of letting you know i wouldn't ever let
go, as if it was possible for us to live day by day
affixed to each other.

a love can only be articulated in so many words
i feel as if i've overused the phrase
and although it will always stand true
there is no new and improved and better "i love
you."

an i love you that tramples all the other i love
yous
a text that can surpass a screen
words that fill you with arousal
a touch that never departs.

i want to scream it at you gently.

i love you.

# future delusion

i sometimes find myself worried about the point in which i entered your life. i am paranoid that time will wear down our love, because while one grows out of their youth, they still have so many opportunities to meet extraordinary people; and with those odds, you would eventually, most definitely find someone better suited for you than me.

when you do, you could put my insecurities on a pedestal, comparing them to the confessed ones of each person you'd be involved with after me. you would evaluate every girlfriend based on their similarity to me. i would be made the reference point for everything you wouldn't want in a relationship.

internally, you would find yourself utilizing phrases like "she reminds me of my ex-girlfriend" in an extremely negative connotation. i begin to wonder if we were to split, if you would spend every waking minute of every hour wishing it had worked out, or if it would actually end up being easier than you thought to get over me. if your comparison of me to others was out of newfound hatred, or simply a tactic to limit remembrance. an attempt to condition yourself to be appalled at anything that resembled me.

the idea of you seeing another woman unsheathed tarnishes my soul; the urgency of you wanting to brush a different hue of hair behind an ear of a different tone of skin, how close you could possibly be to her in order to count all her freckles and bask in her commemorative clear complexion. if her skin was naturally smooth. if she tried her absolute best to make sure every crevice of herself was ready to be received by you.

if i was the only woman on the planet, i would still find a way to make myself jealous.

then, i think, if we were simply not compatible temporarily, if we would be able to reconnect with each other down the line, after an eternity of growth. i ponder if the same flood of feelings would immediately turn in my stomach once you were mine once again, or if i would have to make myself start over, and it would be as if we had never been together at all. if i were to think of all the women you romanticized while we were apart. if i were to compare our second relationship to our first.

if reconciliation can ever truly make up for lost time.

# bitter rain

a happy outrageous fit of confusion
never being able to pinpoint how i truly feel
and why my emotions incapsulate me the way
they do,
rendering me unable to barter with the brain.

pondering everything that could possibly
instigate the swinging of my moods
i cannot plant my feet in the sand and stop the
motion
i cannot differentiate the lying from the telling of
the truth
when someone asks how i am "really" doing.

consistently better but sporadically worse
no more monsoon seasons of ceaseless sadness
instead, the mind drizzles every once in awhile,
naturally amidst the crestfallen seasons,
but if i let it, it transforms into a downpour.

northern cry from the darkest sky
grace my cheeks with your squall of sorrow,
then clear my brain fog, bless me with clarity,
part my mind with your pleasant sun.

let me know that i will make it through
that there are always brighter days ahead
remind me of my past perseverance, shroud me
in warmth
when hiding under the covers of my bed just
won't do.

i am so joyous in comparison to my former self
and yet, her gloom is able to be fortified,
encapsulated,
never to truly be gone
a reminder of her past woes.

# scale your worth

keep the pounds off, baby, you don't want to weigh more than your boyfriend. you want him to be able to take you up against the wall, to hoist you up from the Earth after a long time apart, to be able to count all your bones as an indignant and unspoken form of foreplay.

let the other girls be jealous of your frugality, the frailness of all of you, as if your paper-mache bones will wither and crumple at their touch. let them beg for a form like yours. let them punish themselves the way you have been. let the running of your hand down your protruding spine bless your wrists and fingertips, the showcase of each and every vertebrae reminds us that our teeth must decay in order for us to finally smile at the woman in the mirror. your hip bones protrude as if trying to escape from your pelvis, and your ribcage forms a dauntless entanglement around a heart that has beat much too unhealthily for too long.

the doctor asks you if the recent number on her scale is purposeful. of course it is. i mean, one would have to have a plan in order to look like this, wouldn't they? you wouldn't have worn your dad's t-shirts all throughout your freshman year if you had been pleased with your torso or proud of your chest. you wouldn't have taken more medication than prescribed to you in the morning if it had not been better in comparison to breakfast. you wouldn't have waited all the livelong day only for nightfall when you were granted your first meal, your only meal, in the solitude of your room. you never choose to take a bath instead of a shower, because God forbid you are ceaselessly staring at your legs as opposed to the blank tiles on the bathroom wall.

when you do decide to make the change, there is a part of you that doubts if it will ever be enough. taking "skinny" as an insult now, as a reminder of the way you had presented yourself through minute methods of torture, as opposed to praise, a compliment, a worthy and snide note of envy. your mindset has completely shifted now; you are obsessed with growing and gaining, to make up for all the time you spent deservingly starving yourself.

when people say they do not see a difference as opposed to before, you begin to ponder who you're really doing all of it for. you wonder if there will ever be a happy medium, if you will ever find a median weight that you are finally pleased with, if there will ever be a halt on the maintaining or balancing or calorie counting. you question if there will be just living, away from the numbers, when you ultimately learn to not rely on them anymore. when you trust that your interior is healthy, your exterior is beautiful, and your bones are yours to keep inside of your worthy body.

# woman wide open

do you feel it
the weight of every planet in our universe on
your shoulders.

Andromeda calls to you, my dear,
she wants to tell you that you and her are
expected collide in billions of years
to implode superbly along with the sun.

she has only ever been visible to your naked eye
on moonless nights,
but she wants you to revel, to witness her glory
more frequently than that,
the intertwining of you two able to occur much
more than once a month.

she's even bigger than your inhabited Milky
Way
she's not afflicted with excessive warmth and
turmoil and tragedy
she's not taken for granted.

Mother, you've been treated too unfairly for too
long.

when you finally feel your sweet release
when it just becomes too much for you to bear
you are allowed to crush the everlasting Atlas
beneath you.
relieve Him of his post.

finally join your Earthly hands with your
destined woman, once light years away,
rejoice that she will always appreciate you.
an eternity you will stay.

# human heart

every morning, i wake up wondering what fragment of my soul will shine the brightest today. i wonder how long it will take my heart to build itself back up from her previous night of suffocation and confusion. she wanted so badly to escape from the depths of my ribcage, to profess how much she loved the world around her, and every single beautiful person within it.

she sees the good in everyone. she admires without remorse. she's the girl in class who looks at the girl sitting next to her for just a tad bit too long, questioning the definition and history behind the word "love."

she doesn't understand cynicism, she can't comprehend a constant need to be skeptical, expecting something bad to happen once you let yourself get too happy. for that moment, you are free from your debilitating mindset, the one you formed in order to protect yourself all those years ago. you hope you will grow out of it. someone must teach you to. maybe we'll hug and your heart will get to beat in close contact with mine, and you will start to develop the exact same blissful beat. that will prompt your learning.

i question if the body the universe gave her is enough to sustain all of her emotion. if her unbroad shoulders are enough to carry the weight of her profound world. if her tongue talks in tones fast enough to articulate everything she wants to say, in tune and in time.

one day, i hope she stands in front of those she loves so intensely, finally making it known how much she has grown for the sake of other people. she had to learn to love herself in all her naturality, to resist the urge to transform under other people's pressures.

she knows herself now. her true self. her hands are hers. her arms are stretched out to embrace anyone who's willing to receive them.

she wants to be loved the way she loves others:
fully, intensely, without regret.
without the fear of being shattered.

# stamp of approval

i cannot decide or differentiate
whether i'm a nihilist living blissfully
or an optimist living delusionally,
or a realist cloaked in a fictional haven of
blooming poppies and hot coffees and chocolate
undertones,
vanilla notes and lavender and warm blankets
and steamed mirrors.
the little things always distracted me.

all my angsty letters are water-damaged and
crumpled up somewhere,
i am grateful they are,
i no longer associate myself with the woman
who wrote them.
they were never addressed to anybody,
i thank the universe they were never sent or
received or discovered,
even anonymously.

she didn't have to waste her time
or her blood or her heart or her ink,
she didn't have to appeal to anyone,
give her body up like a provision,
pray to a muted man overlooking her,

shaking his head
tilting his nose upward
only lending hands as she grazed rock bottom
and her arms grew slender and bruised.
skeletal, feminine fingers
branched out, interlocking and wondering and
wishing
for a symbol or a sign to persist.
a signal of beauty and fortitude and forgiveness.

her closet is her confessional.
she is locked in it
talking to herself
and the key resides only in what she will learn
years and years from now,
the indefinite amount of people she will meet
lifting her up like a vigorous weight,
praising her like a false idol,
teaching her like a mother,
disappointing her like a daughter.

# waterworks

the day i cried in your arms was the same day you told me how badly you wanted it to rain; and after that moment, it was as if the sky sealed every last shred of daybreak she possessed as a pardon of your plea. she weeped all throughout the night to the Earth, just like i had to you.

my past weighs me down like gravity, my sky becomes dark if i let it get to me; the forming flood becomes too much for the gutters on the sides of my neighborhood streets. the memories ebb and flow throughout the inner workings of my mind; sometimes they cannot help but spill out towards my mouth, and soon a trail of troublesome tears fittingly flatter the words.

i have tried so hard not to sob in front of my beloved boy. i know the emotion and the reaction is rooted in the very normalcy of human nature, but the vulnerability ventures deep outside my inner comfort zone; as if the feeling is not from within, continuously unable to be contained.

the evening poured oceans for him just like the day had done for my eyes.

he said he would protect me, that he would keep me safe, that although the downpour was debilitating, it was onset from validity and a trauma overflown — not yet overthrown.

no matter what, he promised to stay until all the suns in every universe rose; to wait for the storm to subside, because he knew — through strength — that my soul would shine another day.

# wastebasket

water rings individualize my cover of The
Crucible
because it was the book i always set my iced
coffees on top of.
and i hoped the season would come soon enough
where Starbucks would instead gift me
cardboard cup sleeves around opaque containers,
that they would provide my hands with
much-needed heat amidst the numb and brittle
air.

i wanted to drive to you along the sleet streets
vocal and mobile rain decorating my windshield.
to step outside my car to see you as quickly as
possible,
not the slightest bit worried about my
wide-legged pants getting soaked on the sides.

i yearned to kiss you when it was dreary
when the sky poured endless tears
because i knew i wouldn't care about my hair
becoming frizzy once it dried
or my mascara or my eyeliner running down to
my neck;
i could only possibly be focused on

your cold palms searching for warmth in the
folds of my back.

then, dreamily, you would guide me carefully to
your apartment
pressed firm against me for the journey because
i was so paranoid of falling up the stairs
and i would grant you that hot chocolate i
stopped to get on the way over.
you would take a couple sips of it before setting
it down next to your big red candle,
lit especially for my arrival,
and forget about it until after you were finished
with me.

you would say that you were sorry for not
drinking it quickly, for letting it grow to
room-temperature
and i would think of that as such an unnecessary
apology
because if you had taken your time with it,
you wouldn't have taken me so swiftly;
encouragingly, lovingly, homely, and alluringly
my hands dancing to the tune of the downpour
eyes watering over how much i adored the
feverishness of us two
together.

# to be a woman

to be a woman means persisting with wanting and grace, to interpret her own individualities. it is a vital moment when the jeans that cinch her waist do not dare reach over her thighs, when she realizes her soaked tears are able to make her skin glimmer with a dewlike softness. to be a woman is to be raw and vulnerable, with a still, somehow-closed heart, and damp eyelashes that scooped to the sky like trees bending toward the sun.

to be a woman is a loving torture, to diminish the very beating of a heart and every barefoot step she is blessed to take. every scraping of the knee and the instant waiting and watching until her legs became perfectly smooth again; picking at the scab, and grimacing, not waiting for it to heal.

witness the girl maturing and growing and filling in and spilling out until she bawls.
the generous Mother Earth was a gift, and yet femininity was burdensome to her.
being grounded to her, only her, would never be enough.

women want the stars.

to be a woman worthy of desire is to force a smile to the point of forgetting its fallacy. to be wanted meant to be happy -- quietly -- and to always agree.

and so the aspect would emerge that defines womanhood in all its inherence: she would only cry when the night and all the stars outside her windows beckon it so, when she was truly alone; and when she wasn’t, she would wipe the waterfalls away from her face swiftly before her mother walks in the room, before anyone could have the chance to be worried for her, before anyone would be able to show her that women, too, could let themselves be safe in arms that weren’t theirs.

# deliverance

black velvet touch and gloves worn to prevent
paper cuts
my number-one favorite but never-fully received
prayer:
a sliver of silence amidst a world a little too
loud.

dip powder on my nails so i couldn't chew the
beds until they bled
making sure all my clothes were tight in all the
right places so everyone knew i was still a
woman, even when it was freezing cold.

too soon before, i had hardly ever put my hair up
out of fear of my full face able to be frowned
upon,
and then i spent five years growing it out
because i was finally feminine,
smiling with my teeth because i wasn't ashamed
of the corners of my mouth anymore,
loving fully and finally unafraid of saying
something wrong and being mocked for my
words.

i no longer cared about the consequences onset
by other peoples' eyes.
i outgrew my old ways
my feather earrings and long socks and leggings
under shorts no more,
no matter.

i was finally a new woman
in my hoops and my skirts
my highlights and mascara and seasonal freckles
if i had the time to spend outside,
my snowwhite skin becoming less and less pale
when i basked in the sun.

the marks on my neck
the way i acted before i slept
getting called beautiful and giving my thanks
instead of denying it.

and love,
oh love,
i had finally fortified the feeling for myself.

the mirror glimmered with wide irises and an
embrace
the corners of my eyes crinkled
i was grateful
and just satisfied enough for the care to be
construed as self-confidence.

never concerned as much for my future
as much as i praised the present day.

## spacious

polaroids on my coffee table
birthday cards on my windowsill
the crickets chirp louder than they ever have
before.

in a small little corner of the world
my name is mentioned only in hushed tones
and innuendos
and whispered when i walk past.

traitorous tendencies shadowed by crinkled
smiles
dark eyes twinkling with opportunity
fidgeting hands grasping anything i could reach
for.

open arms to reveal new scars
gracious grievances and appeals to a deity,
praying that the effect he has on me never ceases
as my hands envelop his hair,
twirling brunette strands with my finger.

dear God,
if you really are as omniscient as people say you
are,

please reward me with this eternal love and
fortunate prosperity,
even if insecurity still continues to plague me.

# vanilla and earl grey

vanilla and earl grey,
wallowing away,
hair ties stretched out to become too big on my
wrists.
chai tea, coffee-stained spoons
smeared mascara and the deadline of noon.

lavender and chai,
twelve-year-old me can't bear to say goodbye,
her childhood slips away like the blonde
pigment in her hair.
mirror mirror on the wall
will your weight still fluctuate when you're ten
feet tall?

matcha and pumpkin spice,
the way you speak won't suffice,
the night crawls on like a baby trying to catch a
dog's tail.
and as the world turns a little too fast
all you can do is think about that troubled past.

vanilla and earl grey
i cannot bring myself to say
that i regret every decision i've ever made.

i want to be real-forever blonde and freckled and
free,
fearful to die,
even more afraid of longevity.

# growing girl

as i emerge from my youth, i look back on being
young me's martyr, her scapegoat, both her
excuse and her reason. i wonder if she
remembers crying out of fear of growing up, or
wishing that i would have the answers she
wasn't old enough to discover yet.
i am still trying to figure them out.

i still tear myself down amidst the dead of night
just to build myself back up in the morning,
thinking that i could have been perfect in my
mother's mirror
or the woozy warmth beneath my father's chest.

my presence relishes in a strike of lightning that
touches nowhere, that never stains the ground,
disappearing from the earth without a mark,
never given the chance to pierce a heavenly
body.

i could stare into the sun because i didn't have
anything better to do
and see spots once i realized i'd been spending
too much time wishing i was anywhere other
than Earth.

if i gave in, i could fly.

i could scream in my sleep and have a roommate
jolt me awake
their heart beating a million miles a minute at
the thought of an intruder
when it was just my intrusive thoughts disguised
as dreams, leaping from my mouth and choking
whoever was vulnerable and reachable.

the monsters in my room were real — they were
me. they were the future. they were lost
innocence and looming threats.

the clouds above my head became darker and
the rain upon my scalp became heavier
and i grew the urge to sink into the sidewalk so i
wouldn't be in anybody's way.
watching the world from a tiny crack in the
ground,
a tear in the heart of an inner child that cement
couldn't dare to fill.

# impression to forgive

when i count the thumbtack impressions in my
posters and the freckles on my forearms,
i realize i will never again be freshly eighteen
weeping to the walls of my room because i was
terrified to get older,
or revelating in seventeen because i thought it
was such a pleasing number,
or soaking in sixteen because it was supposed to
be sweet — not confining or isolating or
heartbreaking or nerve-racking, like it really
was.

she shouldn't have to worry about her makeup
fading away with tears
or what to do with friendship bracelets once they
no longer withhold meaning
or choosing what to get upset over and when,
because the heart can only withstand so much at
a time.

she doesn't know that there will come a point
where Christmas morning is no longer worth
waking up at the crack of dawn for
and birthdays become plagued with irritation
instead of joy.

she starts posing for passport pictures with a
grimace
and refuses to jump in any pool because of her
newfound hatred of getting her hair wet.

songs that are supposed to be relaxing are
always sad instead
and the thrill of driving at night turns to a
nuisance before she knows it.

alas, she realizes she's inherited the worst parts
of her environment
an expired product
spending the latter half of her life overcoming
instead of being. instead of appreciating.

and so, maybe, once she learns how to define her
own personal adulthood
she'll appreciate her childhood mindset instead
of resenting it,
and she'll look back on the phases of women
that have returned her stare in the mirror
and thank them all for persevering — no matter
how imperfectly — always extremely
effectively.

# cracked pavement onto red bricks

hell looks an awful lot like my front porch or my driveway
on bad days
i drive like i have somewhere to be
i am unreliable for a living.

i still have the yellow and now-wilted rose my best friend gifted me after a bad weekend
i could never part with it
like i could never part with her,
or so i thought as we both packed our bags to move.

my mom is making me a keepsake box,
it is filled with baby blankets and beanies
and an obvious yearning for me to be a child again,
small enough to pick up and swaddle.

my eyes squint to read smeared cursive writing on old photographs,
the date reading almost-two-decades-ago.
tears slide down the lamination.

i hope the girl in the pictures cherishes her youth
once she possesses her own consciousness.

# sensitive

unable to part with the old pictures that plague
my room
even though i don't speak to half the people in
them anymore.

my old best friend’s polaroid tumbled down
from my wall today,
it slipped between my bed,
i took that as a sign that nothing with us would
ever go back to the way it was.
and i’ve refused to reach within the crevice to
pick the photo back up
because i don’t desire to incite old feelings.
not yet, at least.

too soon to reminisce but too long to be able to
mend,
shared lollipops and platonic kisses possibly
riddled with further meaning
freckles i wish i could steal
first-texts i wish i would still receive.

wondering whether you became too selfish
or if i simply became more irritated.

# respiratory

i have this recurring dream in which i'm holding you in a smoke-filled room; you can feel every inch of me perfectly, but you cannot see any of the awestruck fear across my eyes.

your eyes are watering, i can feel it when i press my thumbs to your cheeks and cradle your temples for a kiss. is it because of the air, or because of your mind, or because of our inevitable demise?

my quality of life begins to decline as my lungs start to strain and fade, but it is all worth it, because my final moment is being shared with the one i love the most.

a homage to the end of our days as i begin to recount everything you have ever said to me. i long for you, even though you are right here next to me.

you hug me ever so tightly, and i inhale in my last breath of tainted air, bidding farewell to all my systems and all my senses.

www.ingramcontent.com/pod-product-compliance
Lightning Source LLC
Chambersburg PA
CBHW051744130826
49812CB00033B/1003
* 9 7 8 9 3 5 7 4 4 2 3 3 6 *